D0194986

THE SECRET LOOK

Other books by Jessamyn West

THE SECRET LOOK
Poems by Jessamyn West

Harcourt Brace Jovanovich, Inc., New York

Printed in the United States of America

The lines from "Vespers" are from *Someday, Maybe,* © 1973
by William Stafford, and are used by permission of Harper &
Row, Publishers, Inc.

Some of these poems appeared originally in *Commonweal, The
Ladies' Home Journal, New Mexico Quarterly,* and *The
Tanager.* The following appeared originally in *The New Yorker*:
"Bee," "Birds," "Cat's Skull," "Chambered Nautilus," "Green
Twilight," "Purely Sabbath," and "Song of Freedom" (as "Song
of the Settlers").

Library of Congress Cataloging in Publication Data
West, Jessamyn.
The secret look: poems.
I. Title.
PS3545.E8315S4   811'.5'4   73–18498
ISBN 0–15–179985–7

First edition

B C D E

You know who you are:
This is for you, my friend
— William Stafford
"Vespers"

CONTENTS

1

2

3

4

1

PRIMARY CATHEDRAL

Primary cathedral, stone's essence, raised
By the hand's gesture in empty air: prized
While the spire was revery and the nave
Dream; the font's marble the delicate curve
Of the eyelid over the covered eye,
Seeing, though covered, the basin's true
Hollowed inversion, the arches that plunge
Upward beyond the unclosed eye's range.

This is my dwelling: the room unobstructed,
Pine corners deploying, perspective as
Deep as the blunt mind can follow. Above,
Knot holes like gargoyles belatedly live:
Are maned horses or little brown bees
That hover unhived. It is built. Its days
Infinite. Bedroom of pine. Not less. Sum
Of all known, room and cathedral the same.

The room running forward to revery where
Nothing is not. Where the ancient spires are.

THE WAVE OF THE FUTURE

The pulse of moving forward
a clock's authentic core
is to the pendulum
a piece of outworn lore.

To forward, forward, forward
he brings his counter revolution;
but clock, implacable machine,
makes backward a solution.

Though pendulum retreat, retreat
with every other stroke
and proudly wag his brassy head
his neck's beneath the yoke

Of forward, forward, forward.
His backward gives the power
that is essential if the clock
should strike a newer hour.

DOUBLE IMAGE

The sea has furrows deep and wide
Like loam the plow has laid aside,
While tree tops have a surf whose thunders
Fill inland air with ocean wonders.

The waves that wash a field of grain
Will make marine a planted plain.
And give a gazer's eye no rest
With watching for a wave to crest.

And that same eye will see as hill
A comber, green and poised and still.
But when it races for the shore
The eye will see, deep in its core,
Those horses foam alone can breed,
The wind drive, and the moon lead.

So earth in sea and sea in earth,
The eye sees double from its birth;
And most delights in what can be
Twin of its own diversity:
The object that is always more
The longer on it you may pore,
Until at last it can contain
The surf, the tree, the wave, the grain.

ALL ROOMS UNENTERED

All rooms unentered wait to hold
the whole of dreaming in them;
in waning light while petals drop
and curtains stir they wait the sound.

What sound do they await, silent
and watching? The sound that you will make.
They know what it will be. Knowledge
infects their corners carnally.

The shadowed keys await your hand
if music be required of you:
the placid glass will break its calm,
mirror your crying mouth for you.

The sound it makes—your crying mouth—
will fill the evening room, will wind
between the slats of chairs, will mingle
with the gloom—if crying be the sound.

Polished, precise, the room awaits:
the listening walls, the whispering flame;
silence will welcome you, echo
your sudden sound and take you home.

WORDS ARE DANGEROUS

Do not play with words.
Say that yellow's life:
Yellow will look back at you
From the dying leaf.

Do not arbitrate.
Say that blue is hope:
Blue's the last that you will see
From a tautened rope.

Don't pontificate
Concerning green and groves:
Green's the color that will surge
Across the shallow graves.

Do not say that red
Is true love's chosen hue:
Red's the color that will flow
When love is through.

If you must choose, take black.
It never did betray:
It always promised night
And death. Not love and day.

AUXILIARY ORGANS

An eye an orb is,
An eye to absorb is,
An eye is where the Lord is:
Seeing, seeing, seeing.

There is His throne white,
There are His angels bright,
There in the eye's clear sight:
Seeing, seeing, seeing.

We but His spies are,
We're sent to cry "Star,"
To Him, else blind and far,
For His seeing, seeing, seeing.

DISRUPTED RADICALLY

Disrupted radically, the thalamus knows
once more the world behind the frontal lobes
free from the superego's pre-made vision:
the thrust of breasts inside brassieres cut to
a cortical constriction.

The mackerel sky
that looks like rain will not bring rain tomorrow.
The thalamus sees the mackerel there and baits
his line for fishing. Disrupted radically
the thalamus eats the jam but will not chew
the label. He tastes the sweet and spews the tag.
Food is his joy, let cortex have the fable.

Cannon for him will blossom buds upon
their stalks of steel. He sees but cannot feel
red flowers that flow where cannon petals fall.

Females as pendulous as fruit he sees
the branch low bending and the harvest heavy:
fingers a pear and parts the hair of the
red-gold whortleberry. And knows that they
suffice, the pear not beauty or the berry
vice.

Disrupted radically, the thalamus thus:
but he'll work back to the cortical sack
and burrow deep in nuances. Bestar
the hood with brotherhood and lighted so
he'll gently go, backward to cortical
pursuances.

THE HELPFUL MIND

The mind must make a trial
Of every kind of death:
Give lungs the chance to feel
How much they owe to breath.

Teach heart how it will be
When blood flows to the ground.
Make eyes, in lightness, see
How death will leave them bound.

Compassionate, the mind
Says, "Children. Thus it is:
Dear heart, dear eyes, dear hand,
Death comes and you are his."

THE REGAL MIND

The regal mind reduced by pain
Must still command a throne,
Although its crest's a rusty stain,
Its language one long groan.

Though sickness whittle down the brain
Until it's thimble size,
The mind beneath its vise of pain
Still scans its one-inch skies.

It makes its kingdom of those things
That once it could not see:
Marks out the single star that brings
The night into a tree.

And turns at last its kingly stare
To what no others prize;
To mark how sweetly, subtly fair
Is all that's small in size.

A spoon, a glass, a curving thumb,
A label's printed letter:
These are its kingdom's royal sum.
It cannot ask for better.

THE SARDONIC WOMAN

A hilltop was the pinnacle she chose
On which to mount her undemanded bounty,
A height from which she saw the night refuse
Her self-known wealth, her great and unasked plenty.

The summer valley lay below in heat
That cried for slaking. Her hands were cool,
Her hair was mist, her whiteness was the
Frost that comes with the first days of fall.

She knew the gifts she bore, the pride of breast
And arms. She knew the coolness that her mouth
Could give. And laughed to think how much was lost
To those who choose, alive, the naught of death.

THERE WAS A CROOKED MAN

Of broken scraggly crooked things
I'll make my self a kingdom
build me a house of timbers warped
and only wryness welcome.

Upon my shelves the books shall stand,
blind rows of that which most should see.
My fire shall arch a broken back
its sullen smoke my comfort be.

Upon my table shattered flowers
shall drop untidy spotted petals;
the dinnerware be cracked and dull
the knives and forks of tarnished metals.

And to that table I shall ask
the spent, the halt, the marred.
Surrounded thus I may forget
that I once walked unscarred.

DREAM

If the cobalt eye on the peacock feather
were not on the peacock feather
but real, horribly real:
if the feather itself were not feather at all
but fissured like flesh whose feel
was real, horribly real.

If it opened and closed and vapored at you
like the lidless eye of adder or viper,
would you say you were dreaming?
If the eye had a beak that feathers had hid,
that pierced until someone (not you) was screaming,
would you waken? Or keep on dreaming?

14

ADVICE TO GOD

I passed an old man
Walking in the rain:
"God bless old men
And take away their pain."

I kept my eyes shut
While I was praying,
But I said, "God, note
What I am saying,

"Note the tender kindness
To a stranger done
And remember our relationship
Is a closer one."

THE SECRET LOOK

"How often now do we see that secret look which
stamps the Elizabethan or eighteenth century face?"

—From a review by Naomi Lewis in the *New Statesman*

Secret to whom, you'd better ask, since Aubrey,
Reading Elizabethan faces, did not see secrets there.
In Bacon's "lively hazel eie" he saw a "viper's stare."
And Mr. Thomas Hobbes, with his "two kinds of lookys,"
Was not thus doubly-hid, but twice laid bare,
As is a writer who does not change his
   story with his books.

We too are secret; but O it takes a better mask
To hide our secrets, when the multiplying air
Can place before the console's million-lidded stare
Our evil hearts. Only the vacant sun-tanned look,
The guise of utter openness, can hide complete despair;
And mask in place, the nervous hands will still
   betray the crook.

16

FOR EVERY FALLEN THING

Cry for joy in April,
Cry for death in fall.
Birth is mother's nuzzling boy,
But death, he loves us all.

Cry for death: the fallen leaf,
The broken web, the frost-numbed bee;
Cry for death: the bound sheaf,
The glazed stream, the bare, stripped tree.

Cry for death, cry for death
For every other fallen thing:
Ophelia's flowers, Keats' tears,
The few gnarled fruits the fall will bring.

Cry for joy in April,
Cry for death in fall.
Birth's an open gateway,
But death's a solid wall.

A COUPLING WEATHER

If breasts could breed, if only they
sweet generation knew, what storms
of cloud, what cupolas, what May
of flowers they'd likely brew.

If eyes could breed entwined as Donne
once saw them long ago, what flailing beams
of light would fall from hazel suns
got when a glance would cling and grow.

If hair could breed, if those small snakes
could hatch a golden litter, they'd move
across the earth and winter break
beneath their surging glitter.

Breasts, hair, and eyes contrive to breed,
to find a coupling weather. They serve,
bound in a sheaf, commingling, their need,
and love, not singly, but together.

GREEN TWILIGHT

Close the door quickly before the green
eye of the twilight insert itself,
shatter with malice the picture you've
made of tranquility. Lidlessly
stare at the fire and the flowers. At the
curtains adrift in the evening air.

Close the door quickly and shutter the
windows. Else evil will enter, will
quietly smile at the pitiful room,
at the hopeful arrangement of
chairs and of books as if time were thus
foiled. As if walls would not fall and the
books lie unread in the unending twilight.

THE DEAD LIMB

Only the dead, gnarled limb
we long gazed on
remains unchanged. Summer
and all of its flowers are gone.
With faces upturned in the mid-morning
sheen we stood. O why did we stare
at a limb coiled in death
when the roses and lilies were there?
"It's the snake in our garden,
a python or cobra," you said.
And now it is coiled there still
while the roses and lilies are dead.

19

THE JOLLY MILLER

The heart that grinds upon itself
Mills bloody meal,
Heaps high the bulging granary
Of horror till

The mind makes bread, crimson and dark,
From this rich store
To feed the heart, that it may grind
Again the fare

Which deepest anguish is to make,
Bitter to taste.
Kind mind to succor heart
With such a tasty feast.

THE ENEMY

We lie together, my enemy and I
entangled bitterly: condemned to lie
like lovers, his gaunt face enlivened by

my living eyes—which watch with horror where
my flesh enwinds him: the living eyes which stare
to see an enemy entwined with lustrous hair.

His smile is wider than my own. His teeth
bisect all pleasures. Smiling, he waits beneath
my flesh the triumph of the cypress wreath.

THE WASTED DAY

Today I pay
tribute to God
and act as if
Eternity

were made and laid
here for my feasting.
Today, a crumb
so small its fall's

not missed, though tossed
by me away.
God's board is spread
to last. Repast

sublime, in time
not ending.
Foolish indeed
is thrift with gift

so wide. I bide
my time and eat
or not. So praise
I Him, and time, His whim.

SUCH COMRADESHIP AS SHAMES THE DAY

You do not cry alone; harken the myriad voices;
your tears are not your own; anguish rises
from the long dead for this day's uses.

No member's wound is singular. No wound
in any part but there were eyes that found
in it the desolation you now find.

Pain has no crevice small enough for you
to fill alone. Its utmost dark will show
such comradeship as shames the day.

They lay in the rye fields through the nights of black frost.
They tunnelled in oubliettes, but the stones held fast.
Their women scanned at dusk an empty west.

The rising wind awakened those who slept
alone. It sounded like the wind in Kent or aped
a voice the years had long since stopped.

Rest now in ceaseless comradeship. They know,
O numberless they know your pain. They cry
beyond the battlements. Their footsteps show the way.

SPRING THAW

He was my winter's pet.
He curved upon my breast of snow
Like purest jet.

Upon my breast of snow
He coiled his subtle winding length,
Both strong—and slow.

His subtle winding length
Lived there as in a crystal cave
And grew in strength.

As in a crystal cave
He lived and never thought of me
Or what I gave.

And never thought of me!
And finally said, "A cave's a tomb."
And so went free.

IF THE KNOWLEDGE OF DEATH

If the knowledge of death were not in the world
could we ever accomplish dying?
Could the body, untutored, lie down and be still,
give over its laughing and crying?

Could silence, untaught, be learned by the tongue,
the ignorant ear forego hearing?
Could the unprompted heart relinquish its love,
be weaned from its hating and fearing?

I practice the art. I lay myself down,
death's silence and blindness assuming:
so schooled my body still finds death
stranger than singing or blooming.

MONOLOGUE

How got you that low voice so sorrow laden?
    I never planned it so.
The lips, whose managed smile, pain more than crying?
The fondling hands whose softness is bone eaten?
    The feet that turn and go?

The voice is mine and yet I heard it laughing
    Short days, or was it years ago?
And heard another voice than mine declaring
Felicities that time has left unproven.
    Who was it planned it so?

OLD MAN STARING: CORNER OF BROWN AND MAIN

She felt his eyeball's rheumy passage
like isinglass upon her leg,
she felt that ancient tapioca lodge
upon her calf and beg
That flesh of hers should have the power
to rinse away his rheum,
to generate again the force that once
invested beauty's womb,
She would have halted traffic where
it flowed by Brown and Main:
if any curve of hers could slay
the years that time had slain.

SOLILOQUY

(young man at a middle-aged gathering)

Come let us strip them back to where
surely there will be found
some core of beauty, seed of grace
about which they are wound.

Unwind, unwind the crepe of face,
the mouths like loving ropes,
eyes that pontificate
severer terms than popes.

Peel back the body's larded hulk,
unwind the unused heart,
uncoil the fingers' grasping clutch,
strip clean each shoddy part.

Far, far within there must be hid,
deep in their center's core,
some grace or beauty like unto
that jewel toads once bore.

28

THOU, SPIDER GOD

Thou, Spider God,
and I, Thy fly,
drawn to Thy web,
afraid to die.

Though dead I'll live,
Spider, with Thee,
yearning to bring
others to me.

AGAINST CLOCKS

The clocks are bleeding time away:
Sweet time, which is our human blood,
They drop in gouts and hourly flood
With chimes our lapsing day.

Bind up the clocks, sever their hands,
Cover the glass through which time bleeds:
Death is the pendulum, his seeds
Darken the lessening sands.

TO DULL BY ANTICIPATION

To dull by anticipation death's pangs—
When the time comes, to say "This is an old story.
This I knew long ago.
All of it
From the first hushed word of announcement
To the final racked breath."

How can it be that there is still agony
In what was so often rehearsed?
Why is pain
Durable
Beyond love and poetry?

The first poem:
Those early words, like doves of light,
Feather-tips exploring the mind's untouched darkness.

The first love:
The lips lifting the body beyond the body's rim.

They are gone
With the quietness of a dream escaped.
While pain, while death
Daily, nightly, hourly, explored, anticipated, accepted,
Sting now as if they were
Wounds
Freshly opened and
Newly bleeding.

SONG OF FREEDOM

Freedom is a hard bought thing
A gift no man can give
For some a way of dying
For most a way to live

Freedom is a hard bought thing
A rifle in the hand
The horses hitched at sun-up
A harvest in the land

Freedom is a hard bought thing
A massacre, a rout
The candles lit at night fall
And the night shut out

Freedom is a hard bought thing
An arrow in the back
The wind in the long corn rows
And the hay in the rack

Freedom is a way of living
A song, a mighty cry
Freedom is the bread we eat
Let it be the way we die

2

AUTOBIOGRAPHY WITH FLOWERS

My cowslip brain, my daisy chain,
sweet nosegay of unreason,
my lily-of-the-valley where
intelligence is treason.

My harebell mind with simples twined
my branch of flowering bane
my garland where the maidenhair
with bleeding-heart has lain.

My garden wrought without a thought
rank volunteer of unwit:
my aconite, my bloom by night
my mourning bride of spirit.

My Venus trap, great botany's map
for planting common rue,
now nightshade's spread and cockscombs tread
where candytuft once grew.

MODEST PRAYER

Dear God please let me see
just once before I die
some ointment that is clear,
completely free of fly.

CLEAN THE WINDSHIELD, PLEASE

Between the world and me
I only intervene.
If I could disappear
Much more could then be seen.

But when I try to vanish
The world goes, too.
My deep opacity is what
I must see through.

ANOMALY

My wicked heart gives me delight;
 Anomaly to see
So mild a face hide from the sight,
 Depravity.

MARTHA KILLED MARY

Martha killed Mary
living in me.
Martha said, "Mary,
put on the tea."

Martha said, "Mary,
there's work to be done.
Close your book, Mary.
It's time you've begun."

"Close your book, Mary,
the sun is now high."
Martha urged Mary,
"Don't stare at the sky!"

Martha urged Mary
from daybreak to dark.
Silent was Mary
as tongue-cut lark.

Silent is Mary.
Closed are her books.
Martha killed Mary
with her hard looks.

Martha killed Mary
living in me.
It's sad without Mary
drinking my tea.

It's sad without Mary,
bitter and sad.
But Martha says, "Mary
always was bad."

ADDRESS TO MY SKULL

Dead, I cannot see you.
Living, you are not.
Curious, unlit lantern,
Carven ivory pot.

On the day they find you,
Ivory damascened
By the grave they gave you,
All your whiteness greened.

Heliograph of horror:
Remember, when they fly,
Once the hands that touched you,
Mouth and brow and eye.

KEATS, KATHERINE

Keats, Katherine, this astringent hour
of sharp sunlight and glittering wind
I willingly subtract from my small store
to put into your banished hands.

O hands that loved the light and wrote,
"I seen the little lamp," feel once again
the gold-leaf weight of gust and sun. Your night
is over long. Take now this hour of mine.

Bright star, be not so steadfast that the sun
can never touch again the hand that wrote
your name. I press into it, out of mine,
this hour of burnished wind and wintry light.

EMILY AND GOD

Emily wanted a voice of thunder
    when she was young:
She with her words of wonder
    like bells rung.

Emily wanted to make God hear
    whatever she said.
Emily spoke out loud and clear
    to Him overhead.

"Emily," God said, "Emily, my dear,
    quiet words
are almost the only ones I can hear."
    So bees and birds

Emily sang and clover and the sea.
    Papa above
Emily told of Earth's infinity.
    And of her love.

When Papa above heard Emily's songs
    jewelled and spare,
"Emily," He said, "my heavenly throngs
    sing not more fair."

EYES IN THE SKY

Eyes in the sky
stars in the grass
eyes to the right
let the stars pass.

Let them march on
battalions of sweet
let the stars scent
the way for my feet.

Let the eyes blink
at stars here below
I'm weary of flowers
let the stars grow.

MICROCOSM

God's minuscule, I'll build a little world, but better,
copied, but clear of what in His is held in fetter.

My little lamp will burn, a sun of kerosene
undimmed by latitude or what the seasons mean.

Snug in the bulging grate the ruddy coals will glow
and heat me more, not less, in time of winter snow.

Symmetrical as God's, the tiger in my lap
is miniature for me and more inclined to nap.

Little but perfect is my world. This only mars:
the kindly walls that shut me in shut out the stars.

FLORAL SUPPOSITION

How is it reported when the day crumbles,
when the night's dust with pollen is scented?
Thus it is said, back of the curtains, over
the flowers: I picked them at dusk. I had
pleasure beyond what is usual. They were
loving as tongues. They fondled my hands.
Dew made them damp. Their skin was like flesh.
I sorrowed to pick them, to see them go limp.

Where the day crumbles, unlit by a lamp,
they say: She was hard to take. She was nimble.
Her flesh was like flowers. I had taken her hand,
would have gathered her, but stayed for a look.
Looking, I missed. She was harvested. Taken
inside by a host, an armload of massed,
dark-hearted ones. Will they care for her? Must
we sorrow tonight for her loss, for her pains?

FAR TRAIN WHISTLE

Far train whistle, needle
Thin, steel-blue in the night,
Stitching us to the past:

Hill curve against a vanished sky
Pepper tree patterns in the dust;
Lock-stitch the heart can not unravel.

WAITER, ANOTHER SQUAB

Eat airiness and swallow grace.
Put iridescence where its light
Illuminates the tomb it falls within.

Great paunch, whose utter night
Has thus a star within its arc,
Once more regale us with the sight
Of tallow's greed engulfing wings
While dentures savor loss of flight.

CHRISTMAS

Now the Christmas barter system
Welcomes Christ to earth;
With tit for tat and card for card
We hail the virgin birth.

We celebrate the holy One
Guts stuffed and wits astray.
God rest you merry, gentlemen
Who mock His Son this day.

CAULIFLOWER WOMAN

Cauliflower woman, mealy and white
Rumpily curved and plumpily tight
Cauliflower woman, do you creamily bite?
If I set my teeth in? Just here? And just right?

Does the curve of the crown in flowers break down
Where cauliflower white crowds the leaf of the gown?
Does grainily cream just darken to brown
Where rumpily plumpness has its renown?

Cauliflower woman most curvily planned
Looped by a leaf and by an eye spanned
Unspanned by the loop of the curvily hand
Cauliflower woman, is it banned? Is it banned?

PURELY SABBATH

Purely Sabbath, fairly Sunday
golden, golden-most un-Monday
God doth wink his topaz eye
twinkle with his lidded sky
wave his whiskered trees about
and Sunday shout, and Sunday shout.

And Sunday shout, and Sunday shout
with his cloud tails hanging out
Holy Sabbath, wholly blest
God doth spend it thus undrest
resting with his Sabbath palms
touching earth with heavenly calms.

Touching earth with heavenly calms
harkening to our Sabbath psalms
flashing all his diamond teeth
on the darkening world beneath
happy that he made this *one* day
purely Sabbath, fairly Sunday.

3

COUNTING OUT RHYME

New as the day star
Old as the night
Far as Orion
Near as a light.
Deep as a wound
High as the sun
Smooth as a stream
Wry as a pun:
Love is all things
Both high and low
And nothing else
Can hurt you so.

TIME IS THE ATLAS

Time is the Atlas death keeps;
bony, his finger points to the edges
of the known lands: traces the ridges
the traveler crosses and sleeps.

Deserts of years and seconds as wide
as a sea, he scans. Only the rivers
he can not ascend. There the lovers
by waters eternal abide.

I ASKED FOR A STONE

The stone I asked
   was solitude,
Clear, cool, and hard
   my chosen food.

They loved me so
   they wouldn't give
The only food
   that I would have.

They crowded bread
   between my lips
They choked me with
   a thousand paps.

Such foods to me
   are purest bane.
My lips long for
   that cool hard stone.

But solitude
   I may not have.
They say it's not
   the food of love.

LAMENT

I loved—the god was mine
and I did eat:
blood warm from his great heart
in mine did beat.

Beloved, I was the god,
the bread, the bride:
and daily was devoured
and daily died.

O let me love again
and no god be;
unloved, but nourished by
divinity.

LAST QUARTER

O little moon that saw our promise given
Beside Benicia's mud caked flats,
After your month of growth and ruin
Behold the work of time and rats.

The leafy refuse which, new born,
You made into a silver wreath,
Now in your dismal waning turns
Rust-red, a circle marred by teeth.

We never saw you full—that hour
When lighted night is nearest day.
Then were there neither silver wreaths nor
Wreckage? Only a little moon lit bay?

PARTING IN RENO

We met beside the station. We cried we'd never part.
    Forevers mingled with the steam
Of locomotives running east and west along the rails
    which space apparently makes one.
Time was forever while space dwindled to a cab,
    a room, a bed.
Eternity was there. And so we missed a sun (it's only
    daily) for all the everlastingness we had.

We slept beside the river in rooms above the water
    to sounds that are forever.
(Since rivers endless run) Surrounded by forever, one
    of us began to shiver.
"It cannot last forever. You are one who must
    confirm a doubted strength by leaving
To try with yet another power (O foolish doubter) of
    further loving."

We parted to the sound of parking meters milked
    in the light of early morning.
The coins came raining down into the hands of cops as
    we kissed, crying.
The tune of nickels paid by men who'd stayed their
    legal limit and no more
Drowned out the sound of Truckee river running
    hard against a stony shore.

TWENTIETH FLOOR HOTEL BEDROOM

Green globed by rain,
shut in a bell
of hollowed green
and endless peal.
Shut in a tear,
a cave of water,
translucent pear
pearl shaped but wetter.
Shut in a womb
of sliding crystal,
we've made the climb
from the world of people.

CHAMBERED NAUTILUS

Our outworn love a chrysalis devised,
a shell impervious to prying:
behind these spirals it contrived
a secret dying.

So private was the death,
so regular the convolution,
they take for life what has
become an institution.

LIKE CLOUD OR STONE

The word exfoliates.
What word?
It does not matter.

Like cloud or stone
It holds
atoms that shatter.

Like breast or star it takes
From love
its utmost meaning.

Sweet feathered word, I'll
Cherish it,
with love's own preening.

ALL DARKNESS IS A BEAUTY

All darkness is a beauty.
All lightness is a duty.

Whatever's dark is made for love.
Whatever's light is made above,
compounded of those atoms God
finds handiest to use as rod.

For light is ice, a coldness never bending
and dark is night, a closeness never ending;
and dark is gentle, soft as shades
while light is sharp and cruel as blades.

Dark is a kindness to enable
starlight to show against its sable;
dark is a river running deep,
dark is a cave packed full of sleep.

Dark is my love. Dark are his hands
and his strange face and those far lands
where he with darkness let me see
how fairer dusk than light can be.

All darkness is a beauty.
All lightness is a duty.

LOVE IN ACTION

Now love in action love in dreams denies,
Pulls down the lighted castle, sends out spies
Who say: too little, or too much . . . or sooner
Sooner should the hands or lips or heart.
Who say: the too large eyes, the life apart.
Who, silent, watch, appraising; twist the word
And bring it back so gnarled its corkscrew turns
Drill inward till the kindled castle burns.

Then love in dreams must build again a strong
But instantaneous vision: massive as clouds, lasting as long
As cloud's duration: which is an eyelid's blink
(In blowing weather, shorter), and live therein
As if such seconds were forever. So win
From time some minutes garlanded with believing;
Sweet castle-love sheltered behind a wall
Which, dreaming over, soon will fall.

EITHER — OR

Two names I've heard of lands afar:
The one's called love, the other war.

Both fables are unto my ear,
The realm of love, the realm of fear.

They say that one has woes untold
They say the other's paved with gold.

In one, deep rivers flow with blood.
The other has a scented flood.

Empirically I'll fix a label:
Call loving true and war a fable.

In dreams, at least, enjoy love's prize
It's not my folly to be wise.

MAD ABOUT METAL

Whatever had wheels or pistons
Whatever of metal was made,
By them they set up their altars,
For them their instruments played.
Sweetly, sweetly, they sang
Their suave little songs to steel,
Piping like crickets from under
The juggernaut's wheel.

Poets with mouths full of rivets
Wounded their soft singing tongues:
Sang bridges and mortars and turrets
And trestles and engines and guns.
The men with mouths full of bullets
Knew nothing of what poets feel.
They sang of women and love—
But never, I think, of steel.

BOMBS AWAY

The earth, from its magnetic core,
Is calling home its own.
Over the arc of earth the call is heard
And the metal sown.

Metal that knew no voice but man's
Knows now another.
A voice that does not call it slave,
But son and brother.

Deep in dark veins the call is made
As earth speaks to her own.
And flying ore goes homeward bound
From every plane that's flown.

THE FIVE SENSES
INTERROGATE THE EXPERTS

"What is this silence?" asks the ear.
"It is the lack of laughter that you hear."

"What is this darkness?" asks the eye.
"A flight of metal birds across the sky."

"What is this odor?" asks the nose.
"The scent a lack of living gives a rose."

"What is this blankness?" ask the hands.
"The place a man no longer stands."

"What can we say?" cry all the tongues.
"We cannot tell you. Ask the guns."

BEYOND ALL METALS

Sea-born and fragile as sea-foam
flesh only can endure;
dark-textured, fabric of earth loam
flesh only is pure.

It wholly is given to living,
it has but one foe;
death's finally defeated in giving
of its pearl-colored flow.

Beyond all metals and their names
it has the power to last,
and will be playing its old games
when guns and swords are past.

4

BIRDS

Birds are a pure
   democracy.
No delegate
   a bird can be.

He sings no anthem
   but his own.
No craft but bird
   by him is flown.

And for his home
   there's but one test—
Has it a curve
   to fit his breast?

No zones to him
   restricted are:
He stamps his foot
   and leaves a star.

It is his sign
   that he goes free:
Is citizen
   of melody.

ROOSTER

Far rooster whose young crow
Is to your throat as thinly scarce
As my words on this winter morning.

Summer shall find us fuller voiced
Your throat, my world crowded with sounds
That say, We are alive and singing.

BEE

Ubiquitous, the bee
is holy ghost to flowers;
the furry gilded dove
of transcendental hours.

Annunciation's heard
where he bores deep:
pollen, the grace he sows
and bloom, the flesh they reap.

BUZZARDS

I walked down to the lupine fields
To watch the buzzards soaring,
To see against the rain-washed sky
Their ancient darkness pouring.
Those birds of death made beauty's self—
Sooty arcs of wonder—
And fearlessly I watched their flight,
For death alone they plunder.

SPIDER

Spider is a herdsman
Spider keeps a flock.
Death is spider's watch dog
Hunger is his clock.

Spider has a pasture
Spread against the night,
Tenuous as star fall,
Terminous of flight.

Spider and his watch dog
Listen to the clock;
Dog all a-tremble,
Spider like a rock.

Spider frees his watch dog.
There's a sound of wings.
Spider puts his clock up,
Quietly he sings.

SLUG

Constrained by fate from being flower
the silvery slug must die;
condemned because a petalled way
enslaves our seeing eye.

He slides like silver on the path,
his stare runs on before;
he convolutes like lily where
he lily doth adore.

But silver, lily, sheen, or life
are insufficient dower
to save the slug condemned to die
because he is not flower.

71

CAT ON SINK

Pard it on moth feet, cat,
Slipper the soundless air.
Let your soft whiskers wave
As if enemies were there.

Rifle the kettle of scent
(The old pot roast's lair)
Four-footed, full-bodied, you
Bring it alive with your stare.

Medusa reversed, you try
The taste of this fare.
O coil your tongue bitterly,
Cat. The kettle is bare.

HEARTHSIDE CAT

In forest aisles the hearthside cat
puts down her feet of moss;
bewhiskered, she looks closely at
that greenly whiskered mass,
the pelt of grass she treads upon
like greater feline's fur:
lashes her tail to frighten it
and looks about with fear.
Her blazing eyes bejewel the leaves
like raindrops after storm;
she brings the forest what it lacked:
the heart beat of alarm.

CAT AND MOUSE

Tib's motherhood extends
Just to her nipples' ends.
Love's boundaries are teats
And what's beyond she eats.

The young of others seem
To Tib a savory dream.
They are not babes to her
But meals done up in fur.

CAT'S SKULL

A cat's skull is the hand's balm,
a shape made for the human palm
a curve for which the hand has craved
beyond the flesh of ladies laved
with sun and air—but bare
of fur. For fur, like hair, will dare
the grave and cushion bone when
flesh is gone. And now as then
fur dulls the skull's stark curve
and makes death's symbols serve
as slope of life's most shining sheen.
And who in watching has not seen
a child's hands in that curved fur
and listening heard the sheathed skull purr.

LEAF USE

Leaves are wind's lips
Full of wind's saying.
Leaves are green strips
Full of wind's swaying.

Tree they abhor
Old earthly anchor.
Wind they were made for,
For him they hanker.

THE EYE, THE EAR

The kingly eye, which can not see it,
Forever seeks its sight.
All else bespeak it
In its fluid flight.

The kingly eye will not admit
That it alone's bereft:
That wind's tones are for
Senses more deft.

The kingly eye forever peers
From its bony socket;
But the wind sits snug
In the ear's pocket.

GREAT WIND I

Great wind, whose blowing can be death,
world gust and my extended breath;
great wind, whose names we cannot say
until our mouths are shaped the way
blowing directs: great wind, we frame
in small your sweep if we but name
Simoon, Samoor, Chinook. We ape,
in Mistral, cold's most biting shape.
Monsoon and Samiel: these too exact
from us fidelity. Compact
decreed by wind when first it blew:
that all its names should bear the clue
of its great strength, its towering might,
its gustiness, its sudden flight.

GREAT WIND II

Like sea it pours but purer,
oh purer much, and clearer
than water which will take the stain
of the leafed pool where it has lain.

Like song it sounds but freer,
oh freer much, and truer
than music's repetitious note,
the sleepy lullaby of rote.

Like sea, like song, but stronger,
oh stronger far and stranger
than they between their shores and staves,
great wind, who music is, and waves.

75

SPRING IN A BOSKY VALLEY

Now trees that were content to let the sun alone,
to stand bare limbed and clean as ancient bone,
must challenge him, take umbrage, run to leaf,
and prove by shadows that they hold the world in fief.

They do. Their point was made a thousand years ago.
Still, they must feather out, expand, grow tassels, show
the sun (and me) that though God said, Let there be light,
tree, too, is great, whose shade can fabricate a night.

For six months now I must contend with leaves for sun,
depend on wind, peer bat-like through the chinks for one
short glimpse of stars. And gratefully breathe what little
air the greedy, multi-mouthed, unquiet leaves can spare.

GREEN DEATH

Green breathes the evening:
The silent breath of dusk
Slides over every face
A mossy husk.

Green breathes the evening:
Exhales those leafy palls
Which seal from sunlight's uses
The faces where it falls.

Green breathes the evening:
Dusk slides in greenness down
The daylight faces sink,
They deep in greenness drown.

SUMMER

Do not beneath great summer's arc
use words to show its burning glass:
beneath the light all words are dark,
and burnished poems, brass.

WALKING THROUGH A MEADOW

My feet are roving clouds
that make cicadas fly;
cicadas are the rain drops;
the meadow is the sky.

A GLASS OF DAISIES

The summer is: three daisies in a glass,
for daisy is the summer's sun,
its burning center and its clouds that pass.

The daisy is: God's eye for seeing earth,
and seeing is a summer sight
of gold dust heat and day's slow flight
across great summer's bulging girth.

God is: the seeing, summer, daisy in a glass;
the summer is His burning center:
and we? The daisy-colored clouds that pass.

MIDSUMMER DAY

One day alone the earth sustains
this pitch of heat and light
then like a mortal easily tired
she turns toward dark and night.

The sun which gives her warmth and life
she can not long endure:
her substance is too grossly made
for element so pure.

One moment only she abides
the sun when he's most gold
then faithless to his fiery light
seeks winter's ancient cold.

We are her heirs. We love like her
but for a moment's breath,
and daily turn from what's most fair
toward the dark—and death.

JULY

On the tongue the day
is a lozenge of light.
On the eye the day
is a pin-prick sight.

In the hand the day
is a nugget of heat.
In the nose the day
is a prickle of sweet.

In the ear the day
is a shout of brass.
The summer sun sets,
day shatters like glass.

TREE BY DAY

A cage by day the summer tree
imprisons tiger sun:
behind her bars his yellowness
is bleached and dun.

She houses him as if he were
no more than linnet's feather:
captive of cage that does not care
for tawny tiger weather.

TREE BY NIGHT

By night the tree a spider is,
tarantula with oaken thighs:
black-haired and poisonous he spreads
across the winter skies;
and has for eyes to menace us
a choice of winter stars:
the diamond stare of Sirius,
the ruby stare of Mars.

EVENING LANDSCAPE

A cone of gnats
a milky way of midges
now constellate the sky
at evening's edges.

The blue-green grass
ruffled, becomes much bluer;
bent low by evening's wind
a blade-sized blower.

Far, far away
there sounds an evening whistle:
down falls the day, down falls
the day spring's gilded castle.

THE HONEST WORD

You write russet, tarnish, hazy, bronze:
Is that it? Have you said the honest word?

You write mellow, moulder, wither, fade:
Is that it? Have you said the honest word?

You write shorter, colder, crystal, far:
Is that it? Have you said the honest word?

You write Orion, frost, the days draw in:
Is that it? Have you said the honest word?

You write a page of words not it:
Then you write death, the honest word.

LATE AFTERNOON

Webbed and banded by sunlight
Swinging intact in a basket
of sunlight; bleached and golden
as autumnal grasses or as pears hanging
gilded with sun-dust in thickets of leaves
the afternoon drowses in meshes
of interlaced light.

Twirled by dry wind, day lapses,
it dwindles toward evening and darkness;
but still the ropes hold, the frayed ropes
of sunlight, still mottled with dayshine,
grapple it closely: the tawny sun-rusted
rope-cradled slow-lapsing full-flavored
late afternoon.

SEPTEMBER

Yesterday the pears were hard,
too green for raiding:
today they're honey in the mouth.
summer is fading.

Yesterday green leaves
mottled the lawn;
now green leaves are russet.
summer is gone.

Yesterday was blade-bright
beneath a metal sun:
that bronze is hazed today.
autumn is come.

Bronze-haze and pear juice,
cold till after ten:
autumn is a new year.
let's begin again!

NOVEMBER

All day you plan the building of
A ponderous, sun-gilt castle;
A dome of bronze where marigolds
Like autumn doves will nestle.

By noon the windows have gone in:
Bright glass as red as adder's eyes
Where you may stand at evening tide
And sulk into the sun's last rays.

At dusk, rococo and complete
Your burnished castle stands;
The lion-legged, dark furniture
Arrives and building ends.

Day darkens, it is time to lead
The somber, ornate life you've planned:
You do not enter, cannot bear
For day's pure light to end.

83

COLD

Cold is a wedge of crystal
between my skin and me,
the thrust of blue-white crystal
where ruby blood should be.

Cold is a tooth of silver
that bites like crimson flame,
a savage tooth of silver
that only June can tame.

Cold is a stare of diamonds
that holds me like a vise,
the bitter-blue of diamonds
transfixing all in ice.

JANUARY

Climate creepeth nearer,
weather nips the bone.
Sharp winter whets his knife
on any handy hone.

He honeth it upon
cat's fur or purple lips,
he honeth it with silvery
slides and darts and nips.

He honeth it until
it flashes northern lights
and spills the frozen stars
of January nights.

Then swingeth it in arcs
that whittle down the sky,
till men look up and say,
"Tonight the snow will fly."

EARTH VOICES

Earth's voice for gossip
    is bees.
For all her sighing she
    uses trees.
North wind is best to make
    a groan,
Wind and old house or wind
    alone.
Earth whispers low with a
    snowflake.
For a quiet smile she likes
    a lake.
Roaring she leaves to
    hurricanes.
Weeping is done with winter
    rains.
Murmuring's a task for a
    summer sea.
For singing she sometimes
    uses me.

WEST, JESSAMYN

Writing my name I raise an edifice
Whose size and shape appear to me
As homelike as the hexagon the bee
Builds for his own and honey's use.

Wasp nest—or palace—is a home
If you're wasp or king. The mole
Is happy in a little hole
And I within my written name.